Ready-to-Use
Graphic Organizers

Supports Balanced Literacy and Cross-Curricular Applications
Grades 1-5

by
Ellen White Holn

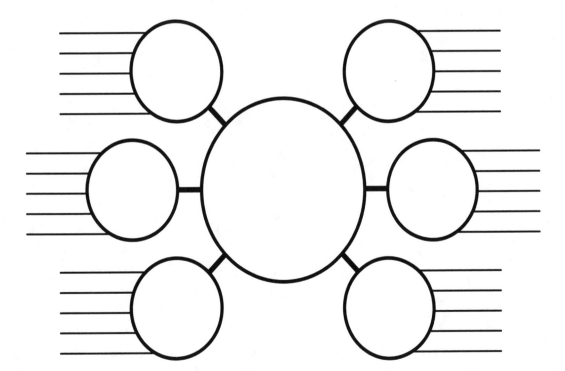

Carson-Dellosa Publishing Company, Inc.
Greensboro, North Carolina

Credits

Editor
Jennifer Weaver-Spencer

Layout Design
Jon Nawrocik

Inside Illustrations
Mike Duggins

Cover Design
Peggy Jackson

ISBN 0-88724-980-9

Table of Contents

Introduction

Whether information is gathered from reading a text, listening to a speaker, participating in an activity, or watching a video, it all must be deciphered and analyzed. A great way to help students process and remember all of the information they receive during their education is to teach them how to utilize graphic organizers.

A graphic organizer is an at-a-glance, visual representation of the important details of a text or topic. This snapshot of information is organized to help students interpret, summarize, compare, or connect information. Because graphic organizers may include written and/or pictorial information, they are ideal for teaching students with different learning styles and ability levels. Graphic organizers are powerful visual tools that can help students focus their attention on key elements in a story, text, or topic area; integrate prior knowledge with newly-learned material; develop thinking processes; and become self-directed learners. Graphic organizers can also help teachers to more accurately assess students by highlighting what students are thinking and how they process information.

Graphic Organizers Included in This Book

Ready-to-Use Graphic Organizers includes the following popular graphic organizers:

- Story Web
- Story Map
- KWL Chart
- Comparison Map
- Venn Diagram
- Time Line
- Chain Reaction
- Paragraph Frame

Although there are additional graphic organizers currently used in the classroom, these eight are the most widely used by both teachers and students. These eight organizers are also flexible enough to be used across the curriculum.

How and Why to Use This Book

How to Use This Book

Ready-to-Use Graphic Organizers provides a wide range of tools to help students and teachers learn about and use graphic organizers in the elementary classroom. The following is a list of the elements included for each graphic organizer in this book, along with a description of how each element should be used.

Instructions and extension activities offer suggestions for using each of the eight graphic organizers. The **Concept** section gives general instructions for use and a brief overview of the layout for that particular graphic organizer. The **Variations** section includes specific suggestions for ways in which the organizer can be utilized across the curriculum. Finally, a selection of **children's books** is listed as suggested texts to study with that graphic organizer.

Sample graphic organizers provide concrete examples of how to use each graphic organizer. From a story map for *The Polar Express* by Chris Van Allsburg (Houghton Mifflin Company, 1985) to a time line on the life cycle of a butterfly, each organizer has a completed example that shows exactly how each element of the organizer is utilized. If desired, copy these samples for students to use as a reference, or transfer the examples to the transparencies in the back of this book to use in whole-group activities.

Black-line reproducibles (a teacher's best friend!) are included for each graphic organizer in the book. Using the reproducible templates can make students' work neater and can serve as a visual reminder for what information should go where. The templates can be used for structured activities in a whole-group setting to review a story or novel, or to prepare for an upcoming unit of study. The reproducibles can also be used by individual students as part of a writing center activity, to prepare a book report or project, or on an as-needed basis, for studying, prewriting, etc.

Color transparencies of each graphic organizer are provided as a time-saver for the teacher. The transparencies can be used for whole-group modeling, small-group work, or individual student presentations. Transparencies are a strong visual learning tool for students who learn in various ways.

Choosing Which Graphic Organizer to Use

First, students should read the material to determine what information to focus on. Next, they should decide whether to summarize, represent, recall, compare and contrast, sequence, or connect the information. Then, students should choose a graphic organizer that will best highlight the information. Next, they should read the description (below) of each graphic organizer to learn which one is appropriate for which use. Note that a graphic organizer can often accomplish more than one of the stated uses, but a main use is listed for each.

A **story web** is used to summarize. Students can use story webs to highlight important sections of a particular chapter, topic, or book they have read, as well as to brainstorm ideas and details for creative-writing assignments .

A **story map** is used to represent. The story map is used to organize the finite literary details of a book, including title, author's name, characters, setting, plot, etc. Completed story maps are similar to old-fashioned book reports.

A **KWL chart** is used to recall. It is helpful to complete with students as they are introduced to topics of study. The KWL chart provides students and teachers with a sketch of students' prior knowledge and areas of interest. This can be useful when developing lessons around students' needs and interests.

A **comparison map** is used to compare and contrast. Students can use a comparison map to compare and contrast several elements of two topics, stories, chapters, characters, etc. This organizer can help students to visually process information and to see the similarities and/or differences that occur between two things.

A **Venn diagram** is used to compare and contrast. It is probably the most popular and well-known graphic organizer. Venn diagrams are helpful for visualizing how two topics, events, stories, characters, etc., are similar and different. These diagrams show connections but also highlight differences in the two areas of study.

A **time line** is used to sequence. A time line is a simple tool for students to use and understand. It can assist students in organizing real or fictitious events in order from beginning to end or from one point in time to another.

A **chain reaction** organizer is used to connect. It is an essential tool in demonstrating how information is related. Chain reaction organizers show how one event or action is tied to, or causes, another.

A **paragraph frame** is used to recall. It consists of simple, open-ended sentences designed for students to record what they learned from a story, event, textbook, etc. Paragraph frames have no predetermined right or wrong answers, which makes them a favorite with elementary-grade students.

When to Use a Graphic Organizer

Graphic organizers can be used at any time in a lesson and with any subject area to help students focus on learning. Graphic organizers can also help students focus their thoughts and ideas during the prewriting process.

The ideas included in this book follow a balanced-literacy approach and are presented for use before, during, and after the reading or presentation of any material.

- **Before reading or presentation**, graphic organizers can be used to help students access prior knowledge, set purposes for reading, and encourage student predictions.
- **During reading or presentation**, graphic organizers can be used to help students actively process and organize information.
- **After reading or presentation**, graphic organizers can be used to summarize learning, encourage elaboration, organize ideas for writing, and assess comprehension.

Benefits of Using Graphic Organizers

- Helps students access prior knowledge and previous experiences
- Actively engages the learner in listening, thinking, speaking, reading, and writing
- Often improves a student's comprehension and recall of a story or subject
- Involves students in predicting relationships and making connections between concepts
- Aids the writing process by supporting the concepts of planning and revision
- Aids in student recall of key ideas and information through visual representations
- Engages individuals, whole groups, or small groups
- Helps with assessments or evaluations
- When used in group activities, improves social interaction and collaboration among classmates

Using Graphic Organizers for Prewriting and Writing Assessment

From helping students generate writing topics to organizing the details of a written piece, graphic organizers are important tools for students to use during prewriting, or the planning stages of writing. Simple, visual planning tools, like graphic organizers, can help students think and plan before attempting to map out complex sentences, comprehensive paragraphs, and longer written pieces.

In the elementary grades, most students will be asked to write four types of pieces: *narrative, informative, descriptive,* and *simple directions.* Following are ways to assess elementary students' use of graphic organizers with these four types of writing. Discuss the connections between the process of planning the writing and actually writing. The assessment examples can also be used as a rubric for students to follow as they complete their prewriting and writing assignments during student/teacher conferences.

Narrative

The story web and time line are typically used when writing narrative pieces. The following assessment tool can be used to assess the story web. Questions for the student and/or teacher to ask when assessing this graphic organizer include:

- Does the center circle name the main subject of the story?
- Are there 3-4 supporting details, listed as one-word subjects, in the smaller circles that branch out from the center circle?
- Are there specific details about each supporting subject listed on the corresponding branches of the smaller circles?

The corresponding written piece should include the following elements:

- Introductory sentence or paragraph that introduces the main subject of the story
- 3-5 sentences or paragraphs that present supporting details or describe what happened in the story (for students in grades 1-2, the piece should contain at least one sentence for each detail)
- A concluding sentence or paragraph that ends the story by solving the problem

Informative

The KWL chart, comparison map, time line, and story map are typically used when writing informative pieces. The following assessment tool can be used with the KWL chart, particularly if the student has completed research before writing an informative piece. Questions for the student and/or teacher to ask when assessing this graphic organizer include:

- Before you conducted research, did you record all of the information you knew?
- Before you conducted research, did you record what you wanted to learn about your topic?
- Did you find out details that you wanted to know? If not, do you want to continue your research?

The corresponding written piece should include the following elements:

- An introductory sentence or paragraph that presents the subject of the research
- 1-3 paragraphs that present information that you knew prior to conducting research and information that you gained from conducting research (for students in grades 1-2, the piece should contain at least 3-5 sentences presenting various aspects from the K, W, and L sections of the KWL chart)
- Concluding sentence or paragraph that states what you have learned and may want to research further

Descriptive

The story web, comparison map, and Venn diagram are typically used when writing descriptive pieces. The following assessment tool is useful when using the comparison map, particularly if the student is writing a piece that compares two events. Questions for the student and/or teacher to ask when assessing this graphic organizer include:

- Did you list two topics, events, characters, etc., to be compared?
- Did you record at least three areas to compare the two topics?
- Under each comparison area, did you record a detail about each topic?
- How will you organize the information so that the reader can understand the differences and/or similarities of the events?

The corresponding written piece should include the following elements:

- An introductory sentence or paragraph that presents the two topics, events, characters, etc., to be compared
- 1-3 paragraphs that list the details of the topics being compared (for students in grades 1-2, the piece should contain at least one sentence for each detail compared)
- A concluding sentence or paragraph that presents why these two topics, events, characters, etc., were compared and/or describes the uniqueness or similarity of the two

Simple Directions

The time line and chain reaction organizers are typically used when writing simple directions. The following assessment tool is useful when using the time line, particularly if the student is writing sequential directions. Questions for the student and/or teacher to ask when assessing this graphic organizer include:

- Did you list the first step that needs to be taken in order to complete the task?
- Did you list at least three additional steps in the order in which they need to be completed?
- Will the reader know exactly what to do and how to do it correctly by reading your directions?

The corresponding written piece should include the following elements:

- An introductory sentence or paragraph that contains the topic of the directional piece
- 1-3 paragraphs that present steps in the order they are to be completed (for students in grades 1-2, the piece should contain at least one sentence for each step necessary to complete the task)
- A sentence or paragraph that concludes the directions and/or tells what the final result should be

Story Web

A story web can help students visualize and organize prior knowledge and important information learned from reading. The story web can also be used when organizing thoughts from prewriting, brainstorming, or when studying.

Concept:

1. List the main idea or topic in the center circle.
2. List subtopics of the main idea in each smaller circle.
3. Write details about each subtopic on the web lines, or branches, surrounding each smaller circle.

Variations:

- A picture is worth a thousand words, so before reading a story, guide students on a picture walk. A picture walk includes viewing pictures, not text, prior to reading and asking brief questions to help students connect what they will be reading to their own life experiences. Before reading, have students complete the main parts of the story web based on their predictions from the picture walk. During reading, ask students to determine the details that describe or define the subtopics and record these details on the surrounding lines. After reading, have students compare what they determined as main ideas from their picture walk with their interpretations after reading the text.
- Have students complete a story web for each chapter of a novel or chapter book. For many children, organizing ideas and thoughts after reading each chapter is the key that links the sections of a story.
- Help students brainstorm before writing. Have the children identify a topic and four main areas they want to share about the topic. Have them record details about each area on the branches. Each subtopic circle and its branches represent the main idea of a paragraph and the supporting details. Have students number the circles to reflect the order in which they plan to organize their written paragraphs. This exercise will allow students to get a jump start on their writing.
- Use a story web as a visual study guide. Have students organize the topic, main ideas, and important related facts from a chapter, a unit of study in science or social studies, or any informational text.
- Work backwards with this creative teaching tool. Fill in the branches of a story web with details about a story or character that the class has studied or a story or character that is well-known or popular. Have students use the details to identify the mystery story or character. This activity can be used to enhance students' critical-thinking skills or as a testing tool.

Great books to use with the story web graphic organizer include:

Frog and Toad Are Friends by Arnold Lobel (HarperCollins Publishers, 1979), Grades 1-2.
The Great Kapok Tree by Lynne Cherry (Harcourt, 1990), Grades 1-5.
Nate the Great by Marjorie Sharmat (Bantam Doubleday Dell, 1977), Grades 1-3.
Stone Fox by John Reynolds Gardiner (HarperCollins Publishers, 1983), Grades 2-5.
Tuesday by David Wiesner (Houghton Mifflin, 1997). Grades K-3.

Story Web

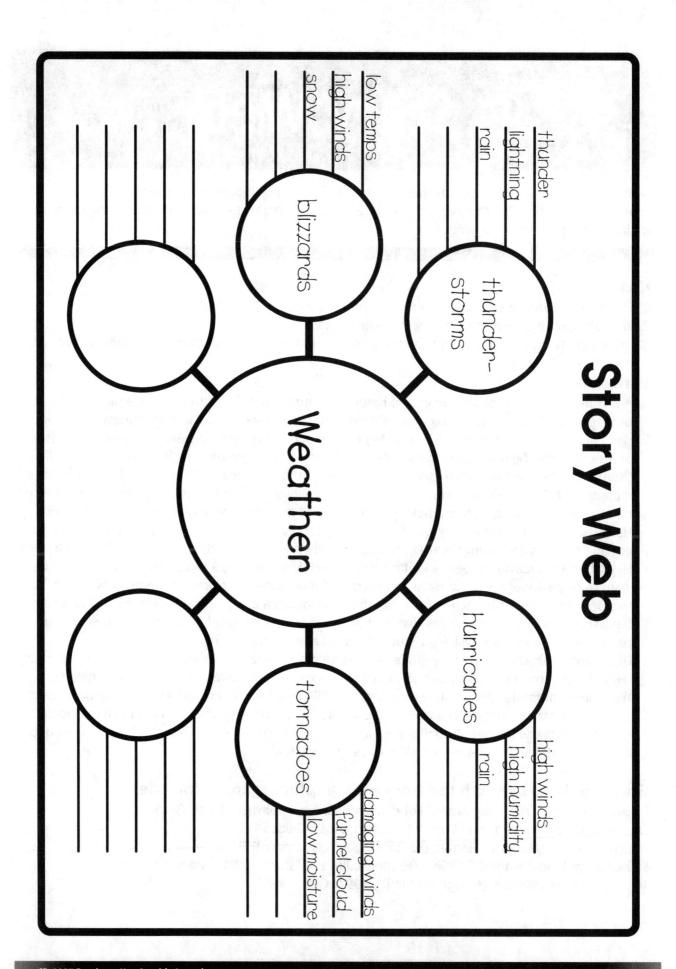

Weather

- thunder-storms
  - thunder
  - lightning
  - rain
- blizzards
  - snow
  - high winds
  - low temps
- hurricanes
  - high winds
  - high humidity
  - rain
- tornadoes
  - damaging winds
  - funnel cloud
  - low moisture

Story Map

Story maps identify the literary elements of a story or text, such as characters, setting, plot, and theme. They assist students in making connections in order to draw conclusions from or summarize what they have read.

Concept:

1. List the title, author, setting, and main characters under the specific headings on the story map.
2. Record the most important details that occurred at the beginning, middle, and end of the story.
3. Based on the beginning, middle, and end details, record a conclusion for the story.

Variations:

- Students' imaginations can sometimes run wild, so use the story map to help students organize their ideas for creative writing. Fill in the title, setting, characters, and the beginning element on the story map. As a class, have students serve as authors and create the middle, end, and conclusion elements on the story map. With student direction, create and write the story on chart paper or transparencies, utilizing the story map elements. Choose a student to transfer the story to notebook paper. Add front and back covers, and place the story in the classroom library for students to read. If desired, type the story and make a copy for each student to take home. Students may also want to illustrate their copies of the story.

- Encourage students to write creative fictitious stories to share with their classmates. Then, let students exchange their stories and complete story maps. Students will easily grasp the concept of publishing when a story map has been completed on a story they have written themselves.

- Help students get their creative juices flowing. In the writing center, place several partially completed story maps with a variety of titles, characters, and settings. At the center, let each student choose a map to complete. Then, have each student practice her creative-writing skills by using the elements presented in the story map to write a creative piece.

- Use the story map to give students a "novel" test. Give students story maps that are partially completed with information from a story or novel the class has read. Have students complete the story maps to test their comprehension skills and assess their understanding of the story and the story map concept.

Great books to use with the story map graphic organizer include:

Gregory, the Terrible Eater by Mitchell Sharmat (Scholastic, 1983), Grades K-2.
My Great Aunt Arizona by Gloria Houston (HarperCollins Publishers, 1997), Grades 2-5.
Officer Buckle and Gloria by Peggy Rathmann (Putnam, 1995), Grades K-3.
The Patchwork Quilt by Valerie Flourney (Penguin Putnam, 1985), Grades 2-5.
The Relatives Came by Cynthia Rylant (Simon & Schuster, 1993), Grades 1-3.

Story Map

Title: The Polar Express

Author: Chris Van Allsburg

Setting:

the Polar Express, a train bound for the North Pole

Characters:

a boy and Santa

Beginning:

The boy boarded a train (the Polar Express) bound for the North Pole.

Middle:

The boy met Santa and was given the first gift of Christmas, a silver bell from Santa's sleigh.

End:

The boy lost the bell through a hole in his pocket, but Santa found it on his sleigh and left it under the boy's Christmas tree.

Conclusion:

All who "truly believe" will always hear the silver bells from Santa's sleigh ring.

KWL Chart

A KWL chart is helpful for students when reading and reflecting on science, social studies, or other informational texts. On a KWL chart, students organize information they **K**now, information they **W**ant to know (or **W**onder) about, and important information they **L**earned after reading the text or researching a topic.

Concept:
1. Before reading or researching, have students brainstorm what they **K**now about the topic of study and record the information under the **K** column of the KWL chart.
2. Also before reading, have students list what they **W**ant to know (or **W**onder) about the topic and record those questions under the **W** column.
3. During and after reading, have students record information that they **L**earned or information that answered questions listed in the **W** column, and record this information under the **L** column.
4. From the public library, school media center, or classroom library, collect books, articles, etc., about a topic of study for students who want to learn more and choose to complete additional research.

Variations:
- At the beginning of a unit of study, let students become investigative reporters to research major topics within the unit. Divide the class into small groups. Assign a topic to each group. Choose one student in each group to be the recorder. Have each group discuss the topic to be studied. The recorder should write information that the group knows in the **K** column and questions about information they want to learn in the **W** column. Have each group research its topic, then complete the **L** column. Each group should choose a reporter to share the results with the class. Display the completed KWL charts throughout the classroom to show students the many topics and ideas that a unit of study presents.
- Make a class book to review and assess what students have learned. Have students choose information from the **L** column on a class KWL chart and write one or more informative sentences about what they learned from a topic or unit of study. Ask students to include an illustration showing what they have learned. Create and laminate a theme-based cover for the class book. Combine the student papers to create the book.
- Tell students that bits of information about a topic provide an overall understanding, like puzzle-pieces fit together to display a picture. Instead of using a chart, record the KWL information with a dry-erase or permanent marker on large laminated pieces of construction paper. Cut the construction paper into puzzle pieces. Have students reassemble the pieces by taping the pieces to the board or floor as they read and review information. Store the puzzle pieces in a resealable plastic bag and place it in a learning center. At the center, students can reconstruct the puzzle and review the information.

Great books to use with the KWL chart graphic organizer include:
Digging Up Dinosaurs by Aliki (HarperCollins Publishers, 1988), Grades 1-3.
Frogs by Gail Gibbons (Holiday House, 1994), Grades 1-4.
The Magic School Bus Inside a Hurricane by Joanna Cole (Scholastic, 1995), Grades 1-4.
Monarch Butterfly by Gail Gibbons (Holiday House, 1992), Grades 1-4.
Weather Words and What They Mean by Gail Gibbons (Holiday House, 1996), Grades 1-4.

Topic: Dinosaurs

What I Know	What I Want to Know	What I Learned
Dinosaurs lived a long time ago.	Why did dinosaurs die?	Most dinosaurs ate plants, but some ate meat.
Dinosaurs were big.	What did dinosaurs eat?	Dinosaurs that ate plants are called herbivores.
Dinosaurs had large bones.	How do we know about dinosaurs?	Dinosaurs that ate meat are called carnivores.
		Paleontologists study dinosaur fossils.
		Dinosaur means "terrible lizard."
		Dinosaurs are extinct.

Comparison Map

The comparison map lets students compare similarities and differences between two topics, and helps students visually organize information. Comparing helps students to better understand the topics, literature, characters, etc., and to make connections between them.

Concept:

1. List two topics, books, characters, etc., to be compared in the two large heading boxes at the top of the organizer.
2. In the center ovals, record the areas to be compared.
3. Research, read, or access prior knowledge and record the details under each appropriate topic heading.

Variations:

- Help students understand the theme of a narrative with an exercise in character study. Have students use a comparison map to compare two characters in a story or novel. Then, choose the areas to be compared. Areas can include personalities, likes, dislikes, ages, etc. If desired, have students use the comparison map to compare one character as he or she is personified at the beginning of the story versus the end of the story, especially if a transition from child to adult occurs within the narrative.
- Take students comparison-shopping. Have students use a comparison map to compare similar consumer products, such as two kinds of bubble gum. Reviewing the products' characteristics, prices, advertisements, packaging, etc., is a simple way to show distinctions between products.
- Use comparison maps across the curriculum.
  - In social studies, have students use the comparison map to compare rural living to urban living, foods of the present to foods of the past, cultures of the United States or Canada to cultures of other countries, etc.
  - In science, have students use the comparison map to compare insects and arachnids, vertebrates and invertebrates, baking soda's and salt's reactivity to different substances, etc.
  - In literature, have students compare authors such as Mother Goose and Shel Silverstein.

Great books to use with the comparison map graphic organizer include:

Cloudy with a Chance of Meatballs by Judith Barrett (Simon & Schuster, 1982), Grades K-4.
Flat Stanley by Jeff Brown (HarperCollins Publishers, 1996), Grades 1-3.
Julius, the Baby of the World by Kevin Henkes (Morrow, William & Co., 1995), Grades K-2.
Song and Dance Man by Karen Ackerman (Alfred A. Knopf, 1992), Grades K-3.
The Teacher from the Black Lagoon by Mike Thaler (Scholastic, 1989), Grades K-3.
The Three Little Pigs by James Marshall (Penguin Putnam, 2000), Grades K-2.
The True Story of the Three Little Pigs by Jon Scieszka (Penguin Putnam, 1996), Grades K-5.

Comparison Map

equilateral triangle	isosceles triangle

3	number of sides	3
3	number of angles	3
3	number of equal sides	2
3	number of equal angles	2
3	number of vertices	3

Venn Diagram

A Venn diagram is used to show similarities and differences between two stories, people, animals, events, time periods, math problems, etc. On a Venn diagram, information is listed in two overlapping circles, with varying characteristics or details listed in the circles and similar details listed in the space where the two circles overlap.

Concept:

1. List the two main topics, characters, stories, etc., being compared or contrasted in the two spaces above the circles. Label the middle space *Both*.
2. Record important details about each that are similar or shared under the center section, in the space where the two circles overlap.
3. Record the main details that are different in the remainder of the circles, under each corresponding heading.

Variations:

- Venn diagrams are excellent resources for comparing two topics prior to and following thematic study. For example, have students compare the Wampanoag to Pilgrims. Have students complete Venn diagrams before and after this unit of study and then compare the differences. Use the diagrams to show students (and parents!) how much students are learning.
- Use a Venn diagram to compare and contrast professions, such as police officer and firefighter. Analyzing the similarities and differences of two individuals, types of people, societies, etc., can be used as a link to the social studies curriculum.
- In the realm of science and nature, animals of the same kingdom are alike and different in many ways. Have students access prior knowledge and research two types of animals that are usually hard to distinguish because of their similarities. For example, students can complete the diagram before and after learning about frogs and toads to help dispel the myths about kissing frogs and touching toads!

Great books to use with the Venn diagram graphic organizer include:

Amber Brown Is Not a Crayon by Paula Danziger (Scholastic, 1995), Grades 3-5.
If You Grew Up with George Washington by Ruth Belov Gross (Scholastic, 1992), Grades 1-5.
Little Red Riding Hood by James Marshall (Penguin Putnam, 1987), Grades K-2.
Lon Po Po by Ed Young (Putnam, 1996), Grades 1-3.
Pink and Say by Patricia Pollacco (Putnam, 1994), Grades 3-5.
Town Mouse Country Mouse by Jan Brett (Penguin, 1994), Grades K-2.

Venn Diagram

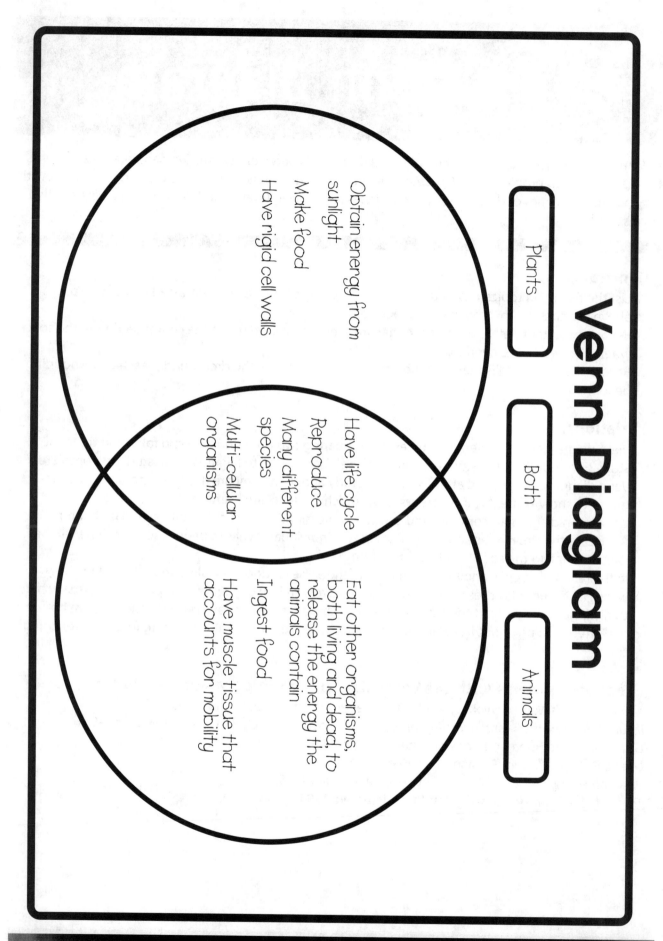

Plants

Both

Animals

Obtain energy from sunlight

Make food

Have rigid cell walls

Have life cycle

Reproduce

Many different species

Multi-cellular organisms

Eat other organisms, both living and dead, to release the energy the animals contain

Ingest food

Have muscle tissue that accounts for mobility

Time Line

A time line can help students understand the most important events within a text, multistep math problems, or real-world situations. A time line can also help students understand events that occur in a certain sequence. On a time line, information learned or noted is listed in sequential order.

Concept:

1. Choose an event, topic, etc., to study. Write it in the subject area.
2. Record the first event in the first section, located on the left.
3. Record the second event that occurred in the organizer section to the right of the first event listed.
4. Record the succeeding events accordingly, or in the order in which they occurred.

Variations:

- Before reading, introduce students to the text by taking a picture walk. Ask students to look through the first few pages of the book or text. Then, ask the class where they think the story takes place and who they think the characters are. Next, ask students to choose words or phrases to identify the first event that they predict will occur and write the words or phrases in the first organizer section located on the far left. Share illustrations from additional pages and have students predict what will happen next. Then, have students read to find out if their predictions were correct.
- The time line and sequencing go hand in hand with this time-line game for center time. On index cards, write important events from several stories. The stories chosen should have been studied or read by students. At a center, have students shuffle the cards and work as a team to assemble the story events together in the correct order.
- Have each student create a take-home book about a story she reads. Fold 8½ " x 11" paper in half horizontally. Layer papers and staple along the fold to create a book. Have each student refer to her completed time line, then write a sentence and create an illustration on each page of her book. Have each student read with a partner, each taking a turn to read her book to the other.
- Use a time line to teach math processes. Have students think aloud and share the steps in addition or subtraction with regrouping, two-digit division, or multiplication. Then, ask students to fill in each step, in order, in corresponding sections on a time line.

Great books to use with the time line graphic organizer include:

The Borrowers by Mary Norton (Harcourt, 1976), Grades 2-5.
Comet's Nine Lives by Jan Brett (Penguin Putnam, 2001), Grades 1-3.
Freckle Juice by Judy Blume (Bantam Doubleday Dell, 1978), Grades 2-5.
If You Give a Moose a Muffin by Laura J. Numeroff (HarperCollins Publishers, 1991), Grades K-1.
Sarah, Plain and Tall by Patricia MacLachlan (HarperCollins Publishers, 1987), Grades 2-5.
Stone Soup by Marcia Brown (Simon & Schuster, 1991), Grades K-2.
The Very Hungry Caterpillar by Eric Carle (Putnam, 1986), Grades K-1.

A Time Line For

The Life Cycle of a Butterfly

Week 1

A butterfly lays eggs.

Week 2

A caterpillar hatches from each egg.

Week 3

A caterpillar is now full-grown.

Week 4

A caterpillar sheds its skin five times during this larval stage.

Week 5

A caterpillar pupates by making a silk-like mat and then attaching its legs to the mat.

Week 6

A caterpillar sheds its skin for the last time, forming a chrysalis.

Week 7

A butterfly emerges from the chrysalis.

Chain Reaction

A chain reaction graphic organizer helps students see the relationship between cause and effect. Students gain an understanding that each action causes something else to happen—every event is affected by the event that precedes it.

Concept:
1. Record the name or title of the subject or story in the title section of the chain reaction organizer.
2. List the first step or event of the subject area or story being studied in the first section of the organizer, located on the left.
3. List each succeeding event in the order that it occurred.

Variations:
- Choose books to study that present material or events that are caused by preceding events in the story. For example, if presenting the book, *If You Give a Mouse a Cookie* by Laura J. Numeroff (HarperCollins Publishers, 1985), guide students to look at the pictures and make predictions about the story, helping them to visualize events which affect each other. Ask students to think about the title of the story and decide what the first action will be. The information should be written in the first section, representing the first event that occurred. After reading, students should record information in each succeeding section that represents the events that took place directly because of the preceding event.
- Nonfiction books about science topics, such as the water cycle or pollution, present excellent opportunities for using a chain reaction organizer. Many natural phenomena occur as a result of previous events. Real-world examples of chain reactions can help students understand how one event causes another.
- Students may also use the organizer to brainstorm *What might happen if…* during discussions about conflict resolution. Use the language-arts curriculum to foster character education.

Great books to use with the chain-reaction graphic organizer include:
The Doorbell Rang by Pat Hutchins (Morrow, William & Co.), Grades K-2.
Goldilocks and the Three Bears by Jan Brett (Putnam, 1990), Grades K-1.
The Great Kapok Tree by Lynne Cherry (Harcourt, 1990), Grades 1-5.
Harold and the Purple Crayon by Crockett Johnson (Dark Horse, 1981), Grades K-1.
If You Give a Mouse a Cookie by Laura J. Numeroff (HarperCollins Publishers, 1985), Grades K-1.
The Little Red Hen by Lucinda McQueen (Scholastic, 1985), Grades K-2.
The Magic School Bus Gets Eaten by Joanna Cole (Scholastic, 1996), Grades 1-4.

Chain Reaction

Air Pollution

_____
_____
_____

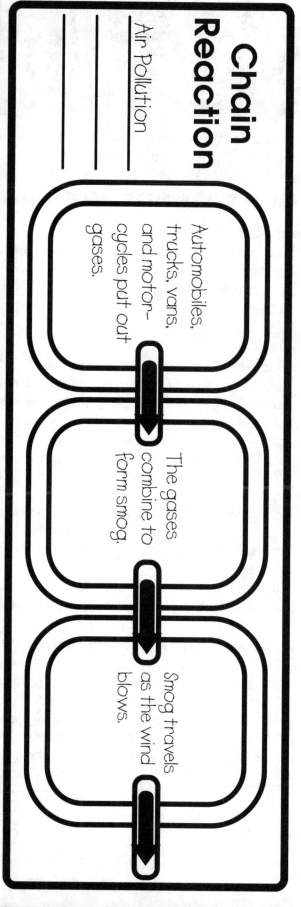

Automobiles, trucks, vans, and motor-cycles put out gases.

The gases combine to form smog.

Smog travels as the wind blows.

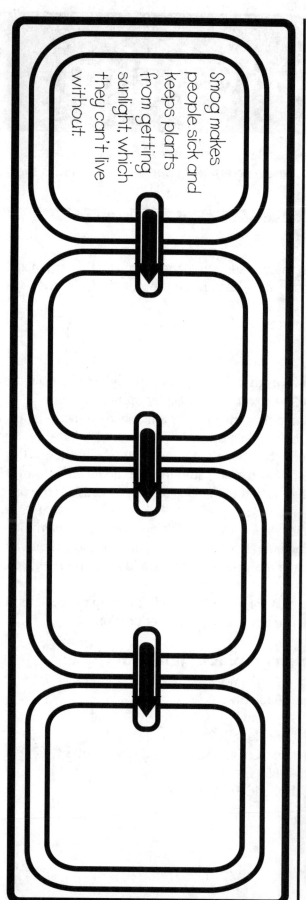

Smog makes people sick and keeps plants from getting sunlight, which they can't live without.

Paragraph Frame

The paragraph frame reinforces comprehension. Young students use this open-ended graphic organizer to mentally sift through what they have read about a topic and condense the information into a few sentences. Because there are many possible answers for each blank on the paragraph frame, most students can successfully complete the organizer.

Concept:

1. Before reading, review the frame with students, explaining that they will read to find the answers to fill in each blank.
2. After reading, have students record information from the text or story. Explain that there may be more than one correct answer.

Variations:

- Reviewing prior information is easily accomplished with a paragraph frame. Paragraph frames can be designed to review important information that students should remember. When used as a test, a paragraph frame can also demonstrate what information has been retained by students.
- Create a paragraph frame to present a star student. Talk to the student before introducing the paragraph frame to the class to find out detailed information which could be included when filling in the word blanks within the frame. After the paragraph frame is filled with information about the star student, let classmates guess the star student. If desired, leave several word blanks to be completed by the class.
- Paragraph frames are great tools to reinforce the concept of writing summaries. Whether it is a summary of a novel or a summary of a guest speaker's presentation, paragraph frames are useful tools for recalling information.

Great books to use with the paragraph frame graphic organizer include:

Brown Bear, Brown Bear, What Do You See? by Bill Martin Jr. (Henry Holt & Company, 1996), Grades K-1.
Caps for Sale by Esphyr Slobodkina (HarperCollins Publishers, 1987), Grades K-2.
The Cat in the Hat by Dr. Seuss (Random House, 1976), Grades K-2.
The Gingerbread Man by Karen Lee Schmidt (Scholastic, 1985), Grades K-1.

Paragraph Frame

I learned a lot about ___the president___

_____. **I learned that**

the president is the leader of the United States

_____. **I also learned that** _the president_

is chosen or elected by the citizens of the United States

_____.

The most interesting thing I learned was _that the_

president is the most powerful leader in the country

_____.

Story Web

Story Map

Title:

Author:

Setting:

Characters:

Beginning:

Middle:

End:

Conclusion:

Topic: _____

What I Know	What I Want to Know	What I Learned

Comparison Map

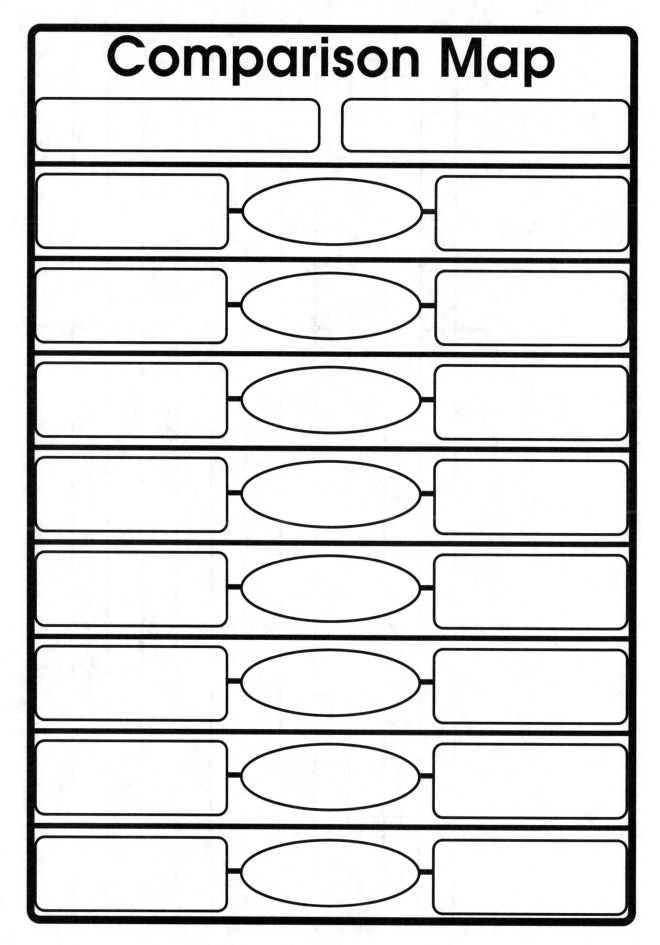

Venn Diagram

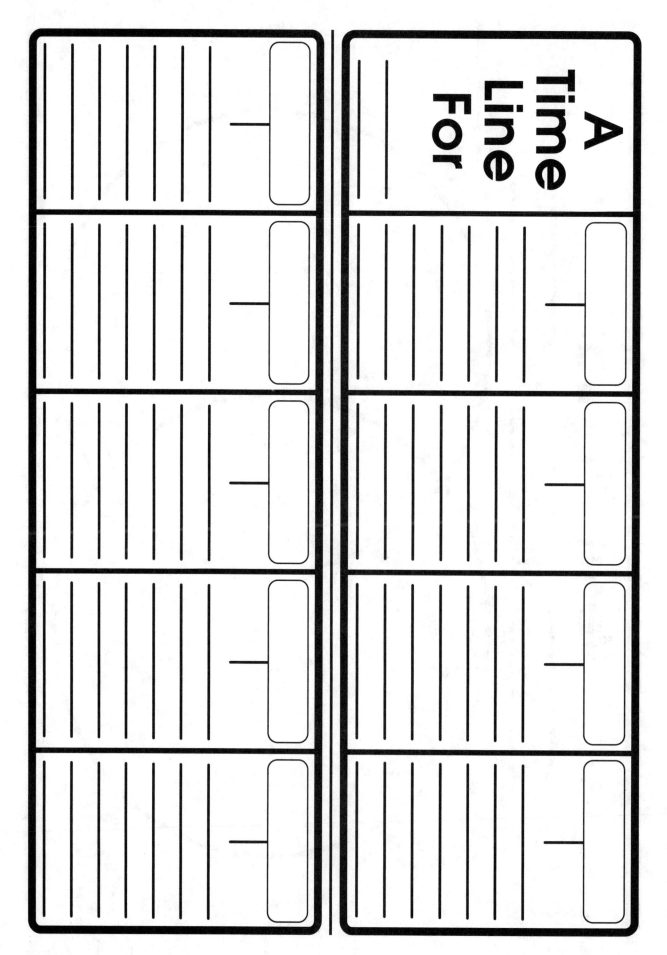

A
Time
Line
For

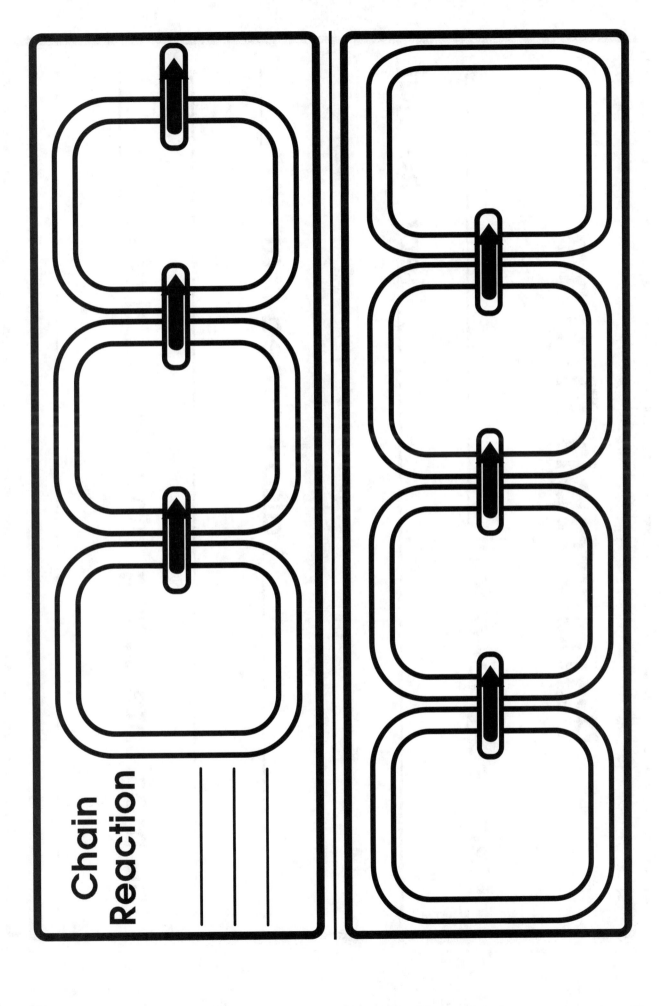

Chain Reaction

Paragraph Frame

I learned a lot about _____

_____. I learned that _____

_____

_____. I also learned that _____

_____

_____. The most interesting thing I learned was _____

_____.